What Happens Before and After Volcanoes Erupt?
Geology for Kids

Children's Earth Sciences Books

BABY PROFESSOR
EDUCATION KIDS

Speedy Publishing LLC
40 E. Main St. #1156
Newark, DE 19711
www.speedypublishing.com

The ground under our feet seems solid, but there's a lot more going on down there than we think! The solid shell of the earth only goes down a few miles and then under that things are hot, molten and sometimes explosive. Read on and learn how and why volcanoes erupt and what happens next.

What is a Volcano?

A planet like Earth has a solid shell or crust. Under that there are molten and liquid layers of very hot rock and metals. A volcano happens when a crack in the crust lets molten lava, volcanic ash and hot gases escape from inside the planet into the atmosphere and onto the surface.

For our Earth, the crust is made up mostly of 17 huge plates that all fit together to make the dry land and the sea beds that we think of as so solid. These huge plates fit together, but not perfectly and they can grind and move against each other.

Where they touch sometimes weaknesses or gaps open up. That's where the lava and other materials from further inside our planet can climb up and force their way out. The movement of tectonic plates is very, very slow. But once a weak point develops, things can change very quickly!

Where are Volcanoes?

Where the tectonic plates are grinding against each other you more often get earthquakes which is bad enough. But where two plates are moving away from each other or crushing into each other, volcanoes can develop.

Under the Atlantic Ocean two plates are moving away from each other making a thinner place in the crust. Iceland sits on top of the line between the two plates and regularly gains land because new volvanoes happen and throw lava up to the surface.

Around the Asian edge of the Pacific Ocean, sometimes called the "Ring of Fire", plates are pressing into each other. As the plate edges buckle or compress gaps can open up—and here comes another eruption!

There are other volcanoes that are not on top of fault lines between tectonic plates. They, like the ones in the Hawaiian Islands, are the result of the action of long-established "hot spots" of molten rock, called magma, under the earth's crust.

Types of Volcanoes

The Earth has been volcanically active pretty much ever since its firm outer crust developed, but not all volcanoes are active at the same time and not all volcanoes look the same. Here are how scientists group them:

Fissure Vents

Fissure vents can be kilometers long, quite low and not very wide. Lava flows out of them rather than exploding upward. Hawaii and Iceland have many fissure vents.

Shield Volcanoes

Shield volcanoes emit lava that is not very sticky so it flows a long way before it cools and stops. The result is a great, flat plain of lava. Many of the Hawaiian Islands are the result of shield volcanoes.

Lava Domes

Lava domes are the result of volcanic eruptions of very sticky lava. The lava does not flow very far from the volcano but rather tends to build it up higher. Recent studies of Mars indicate that that planet may have lava domes as well as Earth.

Cryptodomes

Sometimes when a volcano erupts the lava presses upward faster than the main opening or vent, in a lava dome can handle. The lava presses out the side of the existing dome, creating a false dome that may either explode, break apart or move down the side of the volcano more or less as one piece. When Mount St. Helen's in the United States last erupted in 1980, the eruption created a cryptodome that slid down the side of the mountain.

Stratovolcanoes

Stratovolcanoes are huge structures made up of layers or strata, of lava, ash, rock and other ejected materials. They fit the standard image of a volcano that we think of and they are very dangerous when active. Mount Fuji in Japan and Mount Vesuvius in Italy are examples of stratovolcanoes.

Super Volcanoes

The most dangerous volcanoes are known as super volcanoes. When they erupt they can change whole continents and alter the climate of the whole planet. Yellowstone National Park in the United States is the site of an ancient super volcano that is not active...right now.

Submarine Volcanoes

There are lots of volcanoes on the bottom of the Earth's oceans. In shallower water they can blast rock and gases right up into the air and in the deeper parts of the ocean they discolor the water and send out seismic vibrations that we can track with instruments. Eruptions of submarine volcanoes sometimes result in new islands appearing.

Subglacial Volcanoes

As you can imagine, these are volcanoes under glaciers. When they erupt, lava cools rapidly as it melts the ice and snow above it. The result is a flat-topped mountain or plateau.

Mud Volcanoes

Mud volcanoes can be up to 700 meters tall and as much as ten kilometers in diameter. They are the result of an eruption that ejected more mud and ash than lava.

Before a Volcano Erupts

In the time leading up to an eruption the pressure of magma, gases and lava below a volcano is building up. At the same time a slight movement of one or both tectonic plates below the volcano may give a path for the molten rock and pressurized gases to start moving upward.

Some say birds and other animals can detect when an eruption is going to take place and try to leave the area. Humans are less lucky and often people have very little warning. For example, Mount Vesuvius in Italy was considered an extinct volcano because it had not erupted for centuries, at least. There were villages, farms and vineyards most of the way up its slopes. When it became active in 79 AD, it gave very little warning, certainly not for the people of the time, who were not expecting anything remarkable to happen.

Residents of the cities of Pompeii and Herculaneum did not try to flee the city until the eruption was already under way and thousands of people were killed by poisonous gases or buried under falls of ash and pumice. Pumice is relatively light rock, but it still hurts if a volcano throws it in the air and it lands on you. And the volcano threw enough pumice into the air to bury whole cities.

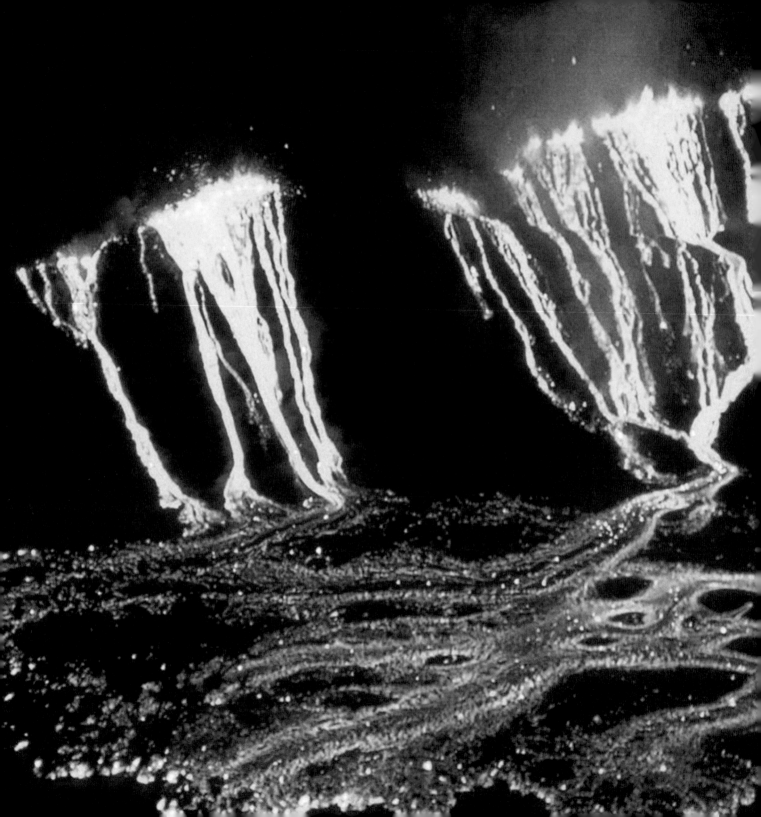

While a Volcano Erupts

When a volcano erupts, there may be a plume of cloud over the volcano. Suddenly, the plume may get larger.

The explosion of lava, ash and rock from deep inside the earth into the air can cause a shock wave that can flatten forests and buildings for miles around and kill people and animals. Debris continues to rain down coating the surrounding area in ash.

More ash can stay in the atmosphere, perhaps so much that it disperses into the upper atmosphere all around the world. This can cause a climate disaster. The sun's light cannot get through to the earth so plants cannot make the food they need.

The earth gets cooler so there may be "years with no summer" which is what happened in Europe and North America in 1815 after Mount Tambora erupted in what is now Indonesia. Acid rain resulting from the debris in the atmosphere may kill fish in lakes, alter forests and open lands over wide areas.

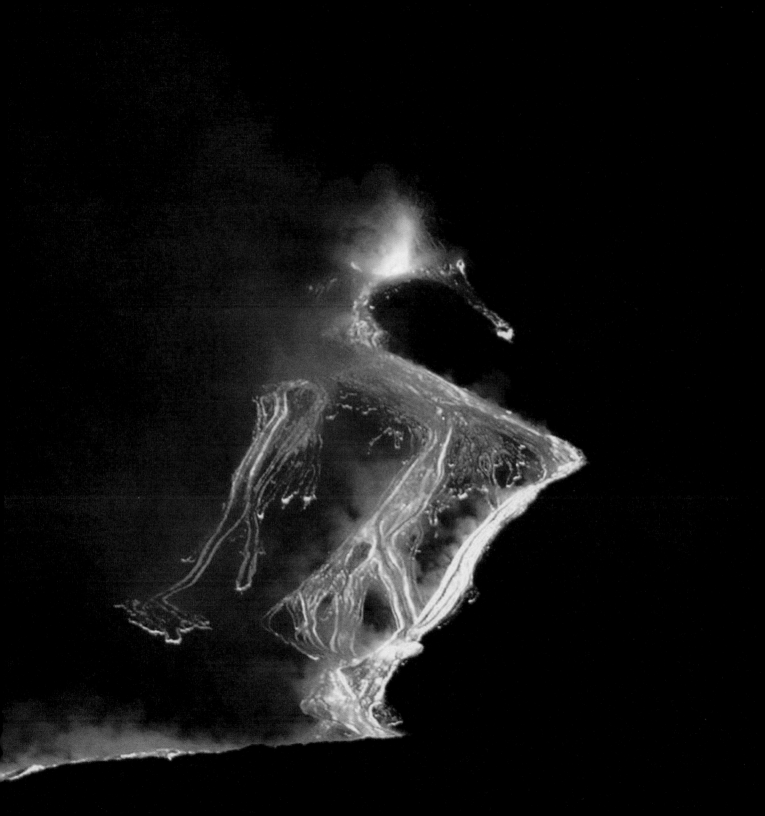

For many eruptions the lava flows out and can travel quite far before cooling and forming into rock. This changes the landscape and can block the channels of rivers.

Some Active Volcanoes

There are volcanoes around the world that are considered active and some are even tourist attractions because they have a continuing but limited flow and eruption of lava. This volcanoes are still dangerous though, because they also emit gases that are dangerous to breathe.

Here are some active volcanoes:

- Kilauea in Hawaii is an energetic volcano with a large lava lake.

- Mount Etna and Stromboli in Italy have been erupting almost continually since people have been writing history.

- In Vanuatu, Mount Yasur has been erupting for at least the last 800 years.

- Mount Erebus in Antarctica has been erupting steadily enough since 1972 to keep its lava lake filled.

- And here's one you probably won't visit! On Io, a moon of Jupiter, the Tvashtar volcano sends a plume of debris and gases at least 300 kilometers up from the moon's surface.

After the Eruption

A volcanic eruption is part of the way the world works. It can be a disaster for humans, for a country, animals and plants but the Earth will recover in time from even a large eruption. The slopes of Mount St. Helens are covered in trees again.

An amazing world! This world is full of surprises, some right under your feet and some in the breezes that blow by you. Look in other Baby Professor books to find out more about everything from rocks to clouds, from seashells to salt deserts.

Visit

BABY PROFESSOR
EDUCATION KIDS

www.BabyProfessorBooks.com

to download Free Baby Professor eBooks
and view our catalog of new and exciting
Children's Books

Made in the USA
Las Vegas, NV
08 August 2024

93537371R00040